CONFESSION
4
POSSESSION

CONFESSION
4
POSSESSION

KAYODE OBIJOLE

PARTRIDGE

To order additional copies of this book, contact
Toll Free 0800 990 914 (South Africa)
+44 20 3014 3997 (outside South Africa)
orders.africa@partridgepublishing.com

www.partridgepublishing.com/africa

DEDICATION

To the Almighty God, who is the WORD that spoke His mind into creation. And to every man/woman who has the same ability to speak the thoughts, desires, goals, aspirations and concerns on his/her mind into existence and manifestation through conscious, deliberate and calculated efforts and methods.

For further enquiries, questions, sharing of testimonies sequel to the usage of this inspired manual or request to Fellowship, Churches, Groups, Evangelical outreaches, please contact:

Opengate Ventures:

E-mail:

commissioned2encourageu@yahoo.co.uk

Telephone: +2349095626923; +2347013705660, or +2348074548381

HOW TO USE THIS MANUAL

1. Have a particular set time and place to fellowship with the Holy Spirit.
2. Take the Manual and open to the prevailing week section.
3. Begin to speak or "lay" the Words for each week / day through a deliberate and conscious declaration on yourself, children, wife / husband, family, career, health. Finance etc.
4. Back up your confession with vivid imagination, that is, see the pictures of your confession on the canvass, or laboratory of your mind.
5. Fertilize your confession with the faith of God to deliver your expectations and living proofs.
6. Keep on thanking God as you retain in your mind the picture of your expectations and desires.

STOP PRESS!

The avenue to achievable outstanding success is not usually a straight one. There is a bend known as failure. A circle called confusion, speed breaks known as friends, red traffic light labelled as enemies, and a caution yellow card called family. You can have a deflated tyre termed unemployment, but if you have an energizing pumping machine known as determination, with a starting engine termed perseverance, an high premium yielding insurance called living faith and a reliably dependable propeller known as inspired confession, it is certainly guaranteed that you will make it to a destination known as success.

For effective, result oriented, proof delivery and Christ honoring testimonies, it is advisable that each weekly confession should cover the entire seven days. The manual in essence is not a once in seven days affairs but a daily bread business of life!. What you voice out with your mouth from this manual must also be in tandem and total agreement with what is in your heart, for whatever occupies your heart and voiced out through your mouth will certainly happen to you now and in a very nearest future. If you refuse to talk, you will certainly be talked upon and or about. If you close your mouth, you also certainly close your destiny.

As you speak from your spirit (heart) the words begin to come out of your body. As you also religiously fully give yourself over and be persistently committed to the utterances of these divinely inspired confessions, backed by the personal conviction, realization and understanding that God has given unto us all that we need to enjoy life to the fullest when He gave us His only begotten son, Jesus Christ, there is assuredly undeniable and unhindered brightness, glory and lifting on the other side of your praise.

We have unshakable faith and confidence in the ability and capability of the WORD who spoke all things into manifestation in the very beginning of creation, that you will never be the same again as you painstakingly by faith lay all these words into your life, marriage, career, business, health, destiny and finance. We are surely waiting for your testimonies on the other side of your praise, and celebration in Jesus priceless name.

Maranatha! !! !!!.

"…..for assuredly I say unto you, that whosoever shall say unto this mountain. Be thou removed, and be thou cast into the sea, and shall not doubt in his heart, but believe that those things which he saith shall come to pass, he shall have whatsoever he saith….." Mark 11:23

"….say unto them. As truly as I live saith the Lord, as ye have spoken in mine ears, so will I do to you……" Numbers 14:28

WEEK 1

I n the name of Jesus Christ, I believe that God's Word is steadfast and unshakeable. It is the power of God, that will deliver me from satanic antagonism this week / today. Nothing good shall be impossible for me. God will watch over His Word to perfect and perform it in my life this week. His covenant over me will not be broken. He will not repent of His divine visitation to me this week / today. My heart will be fully stayed on God's unfailing promises this week. The blood of Jesus Christ will speak mercy, and better things for me and my family this week / today. The keys of God's kingdom is in my possession by reason of my sonship relationship with God through His son Jesus Christ. I now lock poverty out of my career and business. I lock out of my finance setbacks. I lock out lack and frustration from my marriage. I lock out evil set- ups and breakdowns in my health. I deliberately and consciously open up for myself this week / today confidence and understanding by the Spirit of God that dwells inside of me. I seal my confession this week / today with the precious blood of Jesus Christ, in Jesus priceless name I declare. Amen.

WEEK 2

Heavenly Father, I thank you that I am alive in you and socketted to your power and glory. I hereby receive anew dominion and grace by your mercy. Devil has lost the battle over my life, career, business and family. Satanic calendar for my heaven ordained glorious destiny is hereby destroyed. I cancel his evil and demonic agenda over my marriage (or marital plan) and family. The blood of Jesus Christ availeth for me this week / today. I stand on the victory of Jesus Christ that is won for me on the cross of Calvary by His precious blood. I am more than a conqueror in the challenges of life that daily confronts me. I am an over comer over satanic obstacles. I have joy and comfort as a result of God's love released by the grace of Jesus Christ. I have fulfillment and satisfaction through the knowledge of God's Word. Completeness and divine health is my portion and that of my family members. Success and victories are mine in Christ Jesus. Order and peace shall not cease in my life and family this week / day. Deliverance and freedom are my covering cloth this week / today through the shed blood of Jesus Christ. Divine safety and protection will be my reward for serving God faithfully this week / today. This is my declaration this week / today in Jesus matchless name. Amen.

WEEK 3

My heart is fixed on God this blessed week / day. I am indicting good natters from God and men. This is my week / day of goodly and bountiful harvest. It is my moment of divine recovery and restoration of all that the caterpillar and palmer worms of life have eaten. It is my season of Heaven ordained and earth releasing rewards. This is my week / day when every good thing from the Father of glory will lighten my path. I will not walk on the easy short cut road of anguish and despondency. I receive a divine helping hand in the affairs of my life this week / day. I refuse to be a spiritual thermometer that will be soaking heat of life challenges. I reject satanic ordination into stagnation and delays. I refuse to watch things happen by chance in my career and business this week / day. I make things happen by divine enablement and purposeful direction. I will not move ahead of God in any decision of my life, business and career this week / day. I will submit to the direct control and authority of Holy Spirit so that I can have the expected results of Heaven concerning my life and family. I seal up my heartfelt confession this week / day with the blood of Jesus Christ in Jesus glorious name. Amen

WEEK 4

By the mercy of God, I am a beloved child of God. I believe and know that life and death are in my tongue. I also believe and trust that as I make this week / day confession unto life, I shall prosper therein. I stand on the unshaken ground of the blood of Christ Jesus, to proclaim my victory over Satan and his agents. I receive unto myself divine virtues, strength and vigor. I have power and might with ever increasing anointing by the blood of Jesus Christ to deal a heavy blow over satanic gang ups against my life. This week / today Jesus blood will revitalize, reenergize, reinvigorate, reactivates and revive all dead potentials within me. The joy of the Lord will strengthen me against the weariness and weakness of the flesh. His right hand of righteousness will uphold me against the temptations and pleasures of life. His countenance will brighten up my life against satanically engineered obstacles. His horn of salvation and oil of anointing will fan on me like the dew of Hermon. My rod of godly expectations and desires, will pleasantly bud into a tangible proofs of divine fulfillment and glorious earthly manifestations. The desires of mine enemies over my life shall perish over them in Jesus mighty name I confess. Amen.

WEEK 5

This is a brand new week / day the Lord has made for me. I refuse to reap any satanic harvest. Whatsoever that hinders me from greatness before now shall begin to give way. I will no more be debarred from greatness. Every buried potential in me, come alive now by the mercy of God after the order of Lazarus in the grave. Every imprisoned virtue, come forth by the power of God after the order of Joseph in a foreign land. I clear my seized life goods from the ware house of the strongman of my father's house. Every road block hindering my progress in life is hereby cast down with immediate effect by the blood of Jesus Christ. I bulldoze my ways to breakthrough by the power of God. I catapult myself into my desired harvest by the favour of God. The angel of my blessing will not pass me bye this week / day. I will not remain in the land of disobedience to the Heavenly vision. The curse of failure over my labors is broken by the death and resurrection power of Jesus Christ. I walk in the anointing of Holy Spirit to excel and prosper in the affairs of life. My spiritual temperature shall send fiery terror to the camp of my enemies. Evil words spoken against my life in the past shall not hold me captive this week / today. My glorious destiny is released from evil cage of obscurity in Jesus wonderful name I confess. Amen.

WEEK 6

Jesus Christ became poor so that I can effortlessly by grace become rich. This week, I make bold to testify and confess that, I shall not be made a spiritual foot mat for the devil. I shall not become a chess board for satanic games. I also refused to be glued to any problem or challenges of life. I close up every tap of sorrow in my life and family. I stop every shower of pain and anguish in my marriage and health. I block every pipe of shame and ridicule in my business and career. I drink the blood of Jesus Christ as my divine worm expeller. I now by faith expel out satanic worms of delays in my life expectations. I expel stagnation and poverty in my family. I expel disfavor and frustration in my job and business. My enemies shall not triumph over me this week / day. The angels conveying my divine harvest shall not be delayed by the go – slow of life. All satanic laughter at my life will be turned into their sorrow this week / day. All the sorrows of my life shall be transformed into blessings after the order of Jabesh. Every intended failure in my life shall be converted to huge success and breakthroughs. I convert every pain to my gain and pleasure. Every gory tales of Satan for my life shall be changed to glory tales and testimonies of God in Jesus Christ exalted name. Amen

WEEK 7

Knowing fully well that, the weapons of my warfare are not carnal, but mighty through God to the pulling down of strongholds, casting down imaginations and every high thing that exalted itself against the knowledge of God, I confess this week / day that, I will not major in the minors of life. I shall do exploit for God this week / day. I will not be abused by the devil. I will be used by God, to be a blessing and encouragement to my generation. I shall be on fire for God. I shall not be in the fire of Satan nor warm my expectations in the fire of the enemies. I affirm healing and restoration to my spirit, soul and body. I confirm success, breakthroughs and measurable progress into my handiwork this week / day. I eat by faith the body of Jesus Christ. I also drink by faith the precious blood of Jesus Christ with this activity of faith. I disappoint those who expect me to fail this week / day. I refuse to remain today where I was last year. This week / day, a little effort I shall make shall yield amazing results. I will not engage in a labour loss venture of life. I will not embark on a trip that will lead me to self destruction. I shall be adequately rewarded by Heaven this week / day in Jesus Christ sacred name I confess. Amen.

WEEK 8

By a prophet the Lord brought Israel out of Egypt. Also by a prophet God preserved them in the wilderness. By the prophetic utterance for this week / day, my mouth shall only testify the good news of God in the land of the living. I bulldoze every obstacle on my path to breakthroughs. I will realize my set goals by the force of the mercy of God. I detach myself from every vision killer. I disconnect myself from satanic night caterers. I dissociate myself from dream criminals. I paralyze every satanic agent, assigned to monitor the affairs of my life this week / day. I shall not sow for another to come and reap this week / day. I infuse divine life into my systems with the blood of Jesus Christ and the Word of God. I receive divine immunity from satanic harassment as I eat the miracle meal of God's Word. Sickness cannot locate me and my family this week / day. I will not break down this week / day. I shall breakthrough the challenges of life in Jesus name. I am more than a conqueror. I am an over comer. I sing a new song of praise this week / day. My celebration shall not be averted or short circuited. I will be established in good works this week / day. God will be glorified in my life this week in Jesus Christ name. Amen.

WEEK 9

Jesus Christ purchased my freedom, from the curse of the law, by His precious blood. I can no longer labour under the burden of the curse of the law. This week / day, I close down satanic radio station broadcasting evil news about me and my family. My oppressors will be tormented unto total submission. My enemies shall prostrate before me in absolute surrender. My accusers shall flee out of their close places with fear and trembling. Every river from my village mocking the efforts of my life will instantly dry up from its source today in Jesus name. Every satanic case file opened against my life is hereby without delay closed with the blood of Jesus Christ. I dismantle every satanic protocols affecting my breakthroughs. No evil guest will locate my contact address. I withdraw my blessings, from household wickedness. I withdraw my name and that of my family members from satanic surmorn. I withdraw my position from wicked superior in my place of work or business. I withdraw my glorious star from collective captivity. This week / day, no evil shall overtake me. No good shall leave me behind. My hands will not magnetize problems to me. I will not sink in the sea of life. This is my confession this week / day. I shall surely eat the fruits of my lips in Jesus Christ name I declare.

WEEK 10

This is my week / day of transformation. Based on this conviction, my Marah river will receive divine sweetness. My Jericho wall standing against my greatness in life is demolished. My stubborn Pharaoh will drown in the red sea of his own wickedness. My King Uzziah will die for me to experience God's glory in the land of the living. My Herod will be eaten up by the worms of divine judgement. My Harman must hang himself in his own gallows of his evil scheme. My Nebuchadnezar will suddenly change into animal. This week / day, my valley shall become my miracle. My mountain shall become my ladder to divine recognition and prominence. While I am yet living, I will not pick wrong materials from the market of life. I will not lose any ground to the enemy of my soul. I will not be a spectator in the good fight of faith. I will not sell my birth right on the platform of porridge of hunger and weakness. No progress arrester will ever locate me and my family. Every resistance to my breakthroughs will break down by the rain of God's hailstones from heaven. My confession will not turn into my confusion. My heavens shall not become brass this week / day. My wells of joy and abundance will spring up in my deserts of sorrow and lack in Jesus Christ mighty name I confess. Amen

WEEK 11

Father in Jesus name, I declare that I shall be transformed by my confession. This week, my enemies will acknowledge the greatness of my God. The amazing power of God will be revealed in my life. I will locate my divine opportunities. I will leap into favor with God and men. I will leap into unending joy. Every difficult areas of my life will yield amazing testimonies. My week shall not be in struggle and confusion. I will not fall into the enemies trap. Their lying in wait to trap me will be in vain. My oppressor will drown in their own red sea. Those that afflict me shall be afflicted seven folds with divine lice from heaven. I refuse to reap satanic harvest. I withdraw my blessings from satanic banks illegally keeping them. The riches of the Gentiles will be transferred to me. My star will not be obscure in the affairs of life. My star will not be eclipse by satanic wickedness. I cancel any appointment with sorrow. I nullify agreement with poverty. I frustrate fellowship with stagnation. I disconnect myself from disfavor. I will no more take on the title of hardship. I refuse the gift of barrenness in every endeavor of my life this week / day. This is my confession in Jesus wonderful name. Amen.

WEEK 12

The Lord is my light and my salvation this week / day. My oppressor will know that Jehovah is my God. My Jacob will become Israel. The hair of my Samson will grow again. I will not die with my enemies after the order of Samson. My angel of blessings will locate me wherever I may be this week / day. I will not hear satanic noise of fear and intimidation. I will not dance to devil music of impossibilities. I will not sing the Lord's song in a strange land of poverty and disappointment. My head will not be anchored to any evil. My head will not bear any evil burden. I reject any invitation to confusion. I cancel agreement with common calamity. I will not sink in the sea of life. I will not swim in the ocean of problems. I shall not crash in the race of life. God will be God in my red sea situation. The devil will not keep me busy. I will be busy for the Lord. I will serve God with my whole heart. I will not appear and disappear in God's assembly. I will not become a wandering star in life. I will be stable in righteousness. I will be establish in the court of my God. I will flourish in God's vineyard. I will blossom in God's ventures, in Jesus precious name I declare. Amen

WEEK 13

I affirm that my confession this week, shall be a sweet smelling savor in the nostril of God. My destiny will no longer manage poverty. My life shall not be hung on the shelf of regret. My progress shall not be terminated. I will not squander my divine opportunities. My aspirations in life shall not become a pillar of salt after the order of Lot's wife. Satanic siren will not scare away my divine helpers. My life will magnetize favor. Mercy will encompass my life. I will be glued to goodness. I will be a reference point of divine blessings. I will not get stuck on one level of blessings. I will wear the coat of many colors this week / day. Glorious harvest will overtake harvest in my life. Cycle of financial turbulence has ended in my life. Every ordination of debt over my life is cancelled. I retrieve my purse from the hands of Judas of life. The wealth of Laban will be transferred to my Jacob. My Joseph shall not be sold into slavery by the merchandise of household wickedness. The interpreter of my dreams shall not be locked up in the prison of life. My Benjamin shall not be arrested before I see my Joseph. I henceforth reject temporary blessings in Jesus priceless name. Amen|

WEEK 14

F ather in the name of Jesus, I declare that I shall be justified by the words of my mouth this week / day. I refuse to eat the bread of sorrow. I will not drink the water of affliction. The garment of poverty will no longer size me. I will not wear the shoes of stagnation. I will not enter the vehicle of delays. I will not travel on the road of near – success syndrome. I will not rest under the juniper tree of frustration after the order of Elijah. I will not be swallowed by the whales of life like Jonah before I obey God. Satanic attachment of hatred shall not be weaved on the hair of my head. I shall not put on evil lipstick of ridicule. My passion for God will be on the increase. My compassion for man will not lack behind. I will continue to rely on God while I relate with man. This week / day, my life will overflow with goodness. I will be a channel of blessings to my world. I will not be turned upside down by my world. I will turn my world downside up for the Lord. This is my desire. It shall not be cut off in Jesus matchless name I declared. Amen.

WEEK 15

This week / day, I boldly confess that, I am not what the devil imagine me to be. I refuse to be the picture of despair household enemies wished me to be. I am not an image of defeat, I am designed for God's praise, honor and beauty. I am crowned with glory. I am separated from shame. I am disconnected from disfavor. Setback has no part in me again. Disappointment will never locate me this week / day. Evil delays are now strangers to me. Garment of poverty shall never size me in life again. I am cleansed from satanic perfume of hatred by the blood of Jesus Christ. I am sanctified by the Word of God from evil pronouncements. This week / day, I overcome ungodly worry and anxiety. I overcome satanic conspiracy. The snare of stagnation over my life is broken. I am free from oppression. I am escaped from danger. I am delivered from evil obsession. I am established in righteousness. I shall be a spectacle of glory. I will become a wonder to my generation. I am a royal diadem in God's holy hand. I will never be limited in life. I will not be frustrated in my land of Canaan after the order of Jebusites This is my expectation for this week / day and Heaven will sanction it, in Jesus name. Amen.

WEEK 16

In the name of Jesus, I declare my freedom from sin by the reason of the death and resurrection of Jesus Christ. I affirm my liberation from depression. I will not be ensnared by evil association. I am separated from dangers and calamities. I am socketed to God's favor. I am plugged to God's goodness. I am connected to God's abundance. I will command respect because of the grace of God upon my life. I will command attention of people that matters in the affairs of life. I shall be honorably rewarded. Men shall seek to do me good by all means. Favor shall pursue me all about. Goodness will overtake me. I will no more sing the Lord's song in the strange land of complaints. I will not sing the song of jeopardy. I will sing a new song of God's mercy. I will sing a new song of great deliverance. I will sing a new song of divine visitation. I affirm my liberty from sorrow and anguish. I am discharged and acquitted from sickness by the power of the stripes of Jesus Christ. I am released from incessant worry. Doubt is no more my companion. I now have boldness to face my tomorrow because Jesus lives in me. I now have strength and confidence to confront head long my opposition. The Lord shall break the back bone of my enemies, in Jesus name. Amen

WEEK 17

This week / day, my hope is built on nothing else other than the blood of Jesus Christ and His righteousness. By virtue of this, understanding is my portion. Success is my lot in life. Victory is my entitlement. Breakthrough is my birth right. Deliverance is my inheritance in Christ Jesus. My heart is stayed on God this week / day. I shall not fear terror. It shall not come near me. Evil shall not befall me this week / day. Accident shall not be my portion. This week / day will not see my end. If Jesus Christ tarries, I must see the end of this year in peace and not in pieces. I must enter my rest from life's hard labor. I must celebrate God's visitation in my life and family this week. My joy will not turn to sorrow. My celebration will not become a tragedy. I shall not hear sad news. Bad news shall be far from me and my family members. Glad tidings of great joy are my portion this week. Satanic courier vehicle assigned to deliver bad news to me will have its tyres punctured by the angels of God. Only good news will locate my where about. Angelic visitation shall attend my ways this week. I position myself for unending miracles. Ridicule has no part in me again. Shame shall not find me at home this week, in Jesus wonderful name. I declare. Amen.

WEEK 18

Behold what manner of love the Father has lavished on me that I should become the heir of salvation. This is my week / day of fulfilled dreams. I am set for honor. I am ordained for praise. I am divinely composed to sing new songs of transformation. I am divinely plugged to shine for God's glory. I am blessed to be a blessing. I am decorated to attract mercy wherever I go. I am clothed to attract favor. I am empowered to be an over comer. I am crowned to reign in life. I shall be distinguished among common people. I shall be honored above my fellows;. I shall be celebrated when ever men comes in contact with me. God shall do a new glorious thing in my life that will shock and shame my adversaries. New things in righteousness shall spring forth in my business. I will climb a higher ladder of glory in my career. My finance will receive divine sustenance. My spiritual life shall gain new height and deeper insight. My passion for the Lord, will promote my active kingdom participation. The mercy of God will answer for my weakness this week / day. The grace of the Lord shall incubate my life. The truth of the Lord shall preserve me in all my endeavors, in Jesus name I make this confession. Amen.

WEEK 19

I affirm that my confession this week / day shall be a sweet smelling savor in the nostril of God. I declare that through my faith in Jesus Christ, I am a seed of Abraham, and the benefactor of the blessings of Abraham. This week / day, if evil is going ahead of me, God will delay my footsteps. If calamity is coming behind me, God will hasten my footsteps ad this evil will not catch up with me and my family. The light of God is in me, darkness can't abide in me again. Evil can't over shadow me. The light of the glory of God shall be seen over my life and family. Anywhere I go this week / day, I shall always stand out for recognition. I shall not become a wandering star. I will not become history while I am still alive. I shall reign and dominate in my God's given domain. I shall not be dominated. I shall be distinguished for praise and honor. My heart shall be filled with joy. My mouth shall be filled with unending laughter. My heaven of breakthroughs shall open by the mercy of God. The strong hand of my oppressors that is stretched against my destiny shall suddenly wither. I will certainly rejoice over my enemies. There is indeed brightness on the other side of my praise and confession this week, in Jesus Christ name. Amen.

WEEK 20

Heavenly Father, let the words of my mouth and the meditations of my heart be acceptable to you this week / day, in Jesus mighty name. Amen, The abundance of the sea shall surely be converted to me. The nations shall come to me with their treasures. Foreigners shall build up my broken walls. Their kings shall minister to me. The sons of those who afflicted me shall come bending low to me this week / day. Those who despise me shall bow at my feet. I will no more be termed forsaken. I will no more be hated by people who should naturally love me. I will no longer be forgotten in the Lo-debar of life after the order Mephibosheth. Good things of life shall surely pass though me this week / day. I shall eat the riches of the Gentiles. I shall boast myself in their glory. I shall operate at the head only. I shall not operate in the valley of life. I shall dwell on the mountain of praise and victory. I shall not be disappointed. I shall not fail at the edge of entering my promised land of glory like Moses in Jesus name. I shall not be distracted by discouragement from getting the double portion of my desired miracles from God this week. I shall not miss my blessings at the verge of my expected victory. I shall not be dislocated at the point of my desired success. My expectations shall not be amputated by household wickedness, in Jesus glorious name I confess. Amen.

WEEK 21

This week, I trample under my feet, every serpent of treachery. I cancel every evil report written against me and my family. No satanic lies shall prevail in my life. The blood of Jesus Christ is daily answering for every legal demand of Satan over the failures and ignorance of my past. No counsel of the wicked shall stand against me again, because my day of ignorance has been overlooked by the mercy of God. No weapon formed and fashioned against me shall prosper this week/day. Every tongue that will rise up against me is hereby condemned and slashed into irreparable pieces. Every spiritual wall of partition, between me and my divinely appointed helpers, is hereby destroyed by the blood of Jesus Christ. I shall not struggle to eat from the labors of my hand. I shall be honored in the affairs of life. I will not eat from the dust bins of life. I shall not enter the vehicle of delays and slow motion. I will not be beaten by the rain of affliction. Thunder of confusion shall not strike any member of my family. Showers of blessings shall soak me and all members of my family. I am divinely insured by the blood of Jesus Christ. I am safe and secured in Christ. This is my conviction and confession this week / day. It will work for me and I will reap the fruits of my lip in Jesus wonderful name. Amen.

WEEK 22

Jesus is the Lord of my life. I am a joint heir with Christ. I have access to the wealth of the earth, because, the earth is the Lord's and the fullness thereof. Satan cannot deny me of my inheritance that was delivered to me on the platter of the blood of Jesus Christ. The forces of Gentiles shall locate me this week. The glory of God will shine on my divinely appointed paths. The blessings of the Lord will encompass me. The goodness of the Lord shall follow me intimately. The mercy of the Lord shall be my faithful companion. The truth of the Lord shall preserve me from dangers and calamities. The grace of God will sustain me in the heat of life. I am divinely programmed for undeniable blessings. This week, God's Word shall be my delight, because of this, wealth and riches shall locate me by divine emissaries. My righteousness shall endureth for ever. Enduring wealth is my body guard from henceforth. Riches and honor are my inseparable companion. Prosperity shall be identified with me as my heavens of breakthroughs are hereby opened. I am highly distinguished for excellent manifestations of the power of God. So I declare with my mouth and backed it up with conviction in my heart, in the priceless name of Jesus Christ. Amen.

WEEK 23

This week / day, the peace of God that passes human understanding shall keep my heart. The peace of God is my portion because I have peace with God. I will not walk into trouble. I will not leap into danger. I will not sing the song of rejection like David. I am divinely composed, to sing the song of praise. Songs of thanksgiving shall not cease in my mouth. Men shall give good gifts unto my bosom because of God's grace upon my life. I shall attract favor because of God's mercy that I am daily enjoying. I am gracefully decorated with coats of many colors of my heart desires. I am mercifully dressed by God to escape satanic harassment. I will be fulfilled in the Lord this week / day. My colorful destiny shall never be terminated by corruption in the world. I shall be satisfied with abundance. Murmurings and complaints have ended in my life and family. Praise and thanksgiving are now my new songs. Satanic burden over me is lifted and destroyed by the reason of God's anointing upon my life. Yokes of delays are cancelled. Shackles of poverty are hereby broken with immediate effect. I am released from the dungeon of ridicule and disgrace. I am translated into the palace of my glorious heart desires, in the unfailing name of Jesus Christ I confess. Amen.

WEEK 24

This is a brand new week / day the Lord has made for me. My life will surely give a sweet smelling savor of praise to God. I am enriched by God's blessings in all my ways this week / day. Sad occurrences shall not find my life a willing platform for expression. Satanic calendar over my life is destroyed by the blood of Jesus Christ. I am divinely programmed for success. I am packaged for unending wonders. I am designed for graceful amazement. As I build good things of life this week, I will long inhabit and enjoy them. As I plant vineyards of dedication, I will eat their orchard of fruits. I shall not labor in vain again. I will not bring forth for trouble. I am the seed of the Lord, planted by the rivers of His unfailing Word of life for this generation. Before I call God this week, God will speedily answer me. As I am yet speaking to Him, Heaven will instantly respond to my requests. The wolves of life shall not feed on me and my family. The lions of life shall not devour my goals and aspirations in life. Nothing good in my life shall be destroyed on this mountain of faith. My appointed time for enduring goodly harvest has come. I now enter into my inheritance as an heir of salvation of the grace of God in Jesus precious name. Amen.

WEEK 25

This week / day will be a great one for me. It is one that is filled with the glorious expectation of divine visitation. I will rejoice and be glad in it. God will lead me in the path of righteousness for His name sake. Goodness and mercy shall follow me after the order of cloud and fire on the Israelites in the wilderness. Because of this, I cannot walk in darkness. I cannot fail in any good tasks I set my mind on. I cannot be disappointed. The truth of God's Word will change my life this week. It will keep me from dashing my feet against the stone of delays. No challenge is bigger than God's Word. No problem is bigger than the Holy Spirit. No challenge will be bigger than me, because the Spirit of God lives inside of me. God will arise in me by the power of His might this week, and my enemies will be scattered unto desolation. I am God's sheep and I know His voice. I refuse to follow strangers and the wolves of life week. I will walk in God's ways; therefore, my path will grow brighter every day. I will walk away from frustration. I will walk away from confusion. I will walk away from disappointment. I will walk away from darkness. I will walk into the light of God's will for my destiny. I will not be a stranger in my own land of inheritance. Those seeking my life for evil will die while on this evil mission. The wind of glorious change is blowing on me. I am enriched by God's blessings in all my ways. This will affect me and my family for good, better and best, in Jesus Christ name I confess. Amen.

WEEK 26

The Lord is my light and salvation this glorious week. His Word will brighten my path. I am more than a conquerors. I am an over comer through the blood of Jesus Christ. I shall not fear evil for it shall not come near my dwelling place. Terrors shall be far from me and my family. Danger is receiving instant quit notice from the occupancy of my life. Common calamity shall not be my portion. Ancestral curses over my head is hereby broken in Jesus Christ name. For it is written, Jesus has nailed to His cross all those satanic handwritings that were against my glorious destiny. I am therefore disconnected from evil transference. I will no more hear satanic accusing voices. I silence voices of inferiority complex against my life. I am disconnected from the evil of my past by the reason of Jesus Christ sacrifice on the cross of Calvary. I am divinely connected to my colorful future because of Jesus Christ resurrection from the dead. I am free from demonic pollution caused by my parent's religion. Satanic attack against my health is now converted to landmark victory. The hair of my Samson will grow again. The sun of my glory is free to shine brightly now. My dry bone is coming alive now. My Sarah will laugh again. I have back my Joseph as I willingly release the Benjamin of my life to God as a sacrifice. I refuse to be called the son of

Pharaoh's daughter again. I will not choose he pleasure of sin for a season. I choose to esteem the reproach of Christ greater riches than the treasures of Egypt. I am passing through my red sea of life as on dry ground now, in Jesus march less name I declare. Amen.

WEEK 27

I make this declaration in the name of the Lord Jesus Christ this week. All boasting powers assigned against me, is permanently silenced. Every power chasing away my blessing is instantly paralysed. I cut off every evil hand delaying my breakthroughs. My enemies will pitch their tents against one another this week. Evil umbrellas preventing heavenly showers, from falling upon me and my lots, is now roasted by the fire of Holy Ghost. Every power drinking the milk of my life, must vomit them out this week in Jesus Christ name. My locked up blessings are coming out of the prison of jealousy now. I will no more eat the bread of sorrow. I will not drink water of affliction. I will not wear the garment of poverty. I will no more take on the title of hardship. I refuse to wear the shoes of stagnation. I will not take the chieftaincy title of nonentity. I will not be included into the halls of shame and ridicule. I will not become a laughing stock in the midst of my peer group. I refuse to chicken out of life's battles because of fear and intimidation. I am an eagle and I will not flock with chicken of life in Jesus name. I will become the envy of my generation in righteousness. I will be an example of praise and glory to my generation. The Lord shall cause me to laugh again. All the years that locust and caterpillars have eaten in my life is receiving divine restoration right now by the mercy of God. The zeal of the Lord of Hosts will surely perform it to the praise, glory, and honour of His exalted name, in Jesus mighty name I confess. Amen.

WEEK 28

The name of the Lord is like an ointment poured forth. I have faith and absolute confidence in the name of Jesus Christ and in the power of His blood. The anointing upon that name will fall on me and my lots this week. I am anointed to reign in life. I am anointed to be the first among equals. I am specially chosen to be the pick of the pack in my profession. I receive the unction to function in my divine domain, and also to excel far above my colleagues. My divine upliftment this week is not negotiable with the powers of darkness. I shall manifest my full potentials to the glory of God. Perfume of near success syndrome will no longer be sprayed on me. I reject the gift of barrenness in the affairs of life. I receive divine prescription to all my problems. I will not be a creature of circumstances. I will be creator of God's divine purposes. I will add colour and glamour to my environment. I will not conform to the standard of my evil environment. I will be transformed by the renewal of my mind through the unfailing Word of God. I now have the mind of Christ Jesus. Nothing good in life shall be restrained from me to do and or possess. In Jesus name I declare. Amen.

WEEK 29

Father, in Jesus name, I thank you for releasing Jesus from the grave. Jesus, I thank you, for destroying the power of death and hell. By this miracle, my life struggle is converted to prosperity. Evil preparation against my life is hereby frustrated. My enemies must fall into their own traps after the order of Harman. My joy and peace will be multiplied this week by reason of Heaven's visitation. My blessings will be many sided. My life is disconnected from failure at the edge of breakthroughs. I will no more reap any evil harvest in any department of my life. Divine favour is now my lot in life. I am cut off from inherited poverty. The resurrection of Jesus Christ has repaired any faulty foundation of my life. This week, my life must carry divine prosperity. I shall not offer unacceptable offerings unto the Lord by my ways and attitudes. I shall not slow down God with my unbelief. I will not harbor any prayer killer in my life. I refuse to ask God anything contrary to His will. My prayers shall not enter voice mail of complaints. God's praise on the network of my lips shall not be jammed by heavy traffic of carnal murmurings. I shall never access satanic network in place of God's saving avenues of Jesus Christ. I am tied up for the Master's use like the colt that Jesus Christ rode triumphantly into Jerusalem. God must be glorified in my life this week, in Jesus mighty name I declare. Amen.

WEEK 30

It is written, at the name of Jesus Christ, every knee should bow. I key into this understanding and declare that, no satanic dustbin fashioned against me and my family shall prosper. I recover every fragment of my life from the hands of household wickedness. I am set free from every evil grip of household manipulations. I over throw demonic judgement directed against my glory. I dismantle evil throne installed against my advancement. I challenge and disgrace satanic prophets, hired against my life and career. I over throw evil authority backing up my enemies. I command the source of the strength of my adversaries to dry up by fire. The foot hold of satanic oppressors against my life will become slippery in Jesus Christ name. I remove every garment of reproach in my life. I refuse evil design and label placed upon my life. This week, riot and confusion shall baptize the camp of my enemies. The aeroplane harbouring my enemies will crash land in the "Lisa Village" of life. The evil pipe draining away my virtues will burst open by fire in Jesus name. The evil eyes assigned to monitor my progress in life must receive total blindness now. This is my week of rest and peace in Jesus Christ mighty name I declare. Amen.

WEEK 31

This week, I exercise my dominion as a child of the Most High God. I close down satanic broadcasting station fashioned against me and my family. I dismantle demonic opposition to my breakthroughs. I am released from anti-excellence spirit. Every satanic case file against my destiny is closed by the blood of Jesus Christ. My foes will prostrate before me in total surrender. Evil river from my village that is mocking the efforts of my life, must dry up from its source now in Jesus Christ name. Evil guests shall not locate my residence. No grave will hold captives my miracles again in life. My mountains have become my miracles. I will not become a reference point for evil in my generation. I will no longer pick the wrong materials from the market of life. My prosperity will not become history, while I am still living. I paralyse the activities of progress arresters. My breakthroughs this week shall baffle my detractors. My attackers shall be attacked by the military angels of God. I cut off supply of food to my challengers. I destroy the pillar of strength that is backing my detractors. I am released from known and unknown curses by the blood of Jesus Christ. I divide the tongue of the congregation of darkness against my destiny after the order of Babel, in Jesus Christ name I make this confession. Amen.

WEEK 32

Father, in Jesus Christ name, as truly as You live, I thank You because You will do, whatever I speak now in Your ears. This week, by my words of confession, I frame my world of peace and good order. By my utterances, I fashion my world of abundance and fulfillment. I will offer unto God, a more excellent sacrifice of praise. Every dead potential in me will speak out again!. I am translated into a glorious relationship with my Maker. I will not be found among the dead. I will not sojourned as s stranger, in my land of promise. I will no longer dwell in the tabernacle of shame. I will no more worship the true and living God in the synagogue of ridicule. I will not sing the Lord's song in the land of rejection. I will not dance to the music of my oppressors. I will not become a spectacle of ridicule in the stadium of my adversaries after the order of Samson. I will not lose the strength of my life on the laps of Delilahs of life. I will not be trapped by the evil antics of Portiphar's wife. I will not sell my glorious birthright at the instance of enticing porridge of my enemies. I will not rush ahead of God's plan to produce satanic Ishmeal instead of my promised Isaac. This week, I receive divine enablement to conceive godly ideas. I will deliver a generational impact visions. In Jesus Christ matchless name I declare. Amen.

WEEK 33

I affirm that in this brand new week, I am a proper child of God. This is the reason why God has been keeping me safe since I was born like Moses who was kept by his parent. I refuse to be called the son of Pharaoh's daughter. I will not be bed ridden in the red sea of life. I am passing through my red sea now as by dry land. I pull down the walls of my Jericho. I compass them round about now with my song of praise and worship. I will not perish with my enemies like Samson. I subdue the kingdom of delays by the mercy of God. I overthrow the kingdom of poverty by the death and resurrection of Jesus Christ. I wrought righteousness by the faith of God. I will obtain promises of expansions. I quench the violence fire of disappointment. I escape the edge of the sword of sorrows and calamities. Out of weakness in the battle of life, I am now made strong by the victory of Jesus Christ on the cross of Calvary. I will wax valiant in the fight of faith. I turn to flight the armies of conspiracy against my glorious destiny. My desires shall not die as I wait in hope. I will no more see the promises of God afar off again like Moses. I must partake in God's goodness in the land of the living this week in Jesus precious name. Amen.

WEEK 34

Jesus Christ paid the price for the debt of sin I could never pay. He was bruised for my wrong doings in life, therefore, this week, I confess that, I will no more be subjected into trials of cruel mocking. I will not be stranded in the dens of forgetfulness. I will not be pestered with the stone of poverty. I receive my dead blessings raise to life again by the same power that raised up Jesus Christ. My testimonies shall never be sawn asunder by the conspiracy of dark powers. The sword of the wicked will not slay me and any member of my family. I will not wander about life in sheepskins of frustration. I will not roam about aimlessly in life issues in goat skins of stubbornness. I will not wander in the desert of unproductivity. I shall not become destitute in the affairs of life. I will no longer be fed by demonic night caterers. I shall not be corrupted by satanic dream criminals. My tormentors shall be tormented unto total surrender. My enemies shall be boxed into the corner of disappointment. I will not be forgotten in the caves of obscurity. I will not be forgotten in the prison of evil conspiracy by my divine helpers after the order of Joseph. I will obtain good report through my heartily confession. I will receive the promise of better things this glorious week, in Jesus mighty name I declare. Amen.

WEEK 35

Father, in Jesus Christ name, I thank you because You are faithful, to give expression to my confession. I declare that Satan has no power over me and my family this week. Agents of frustration has no control over my career and health. Agents of poverty shall not locate me. I am removed from the influence of spiritual rags. Agents of defeat has no hold over me again. I am disconnected from infirmity. I set on fire every instrument of darkness fashioned against my life. I release heavenly virus on all satanic computers fashioned against my destiny. I disconnect devilish satellites, been used to manipulate me and my family. I destroy satanic cameras been used to monitor my life. I break evil web-cam been used to view my marital status. I break satanic thermometer been used to gauge my spiritual life. I release leprosy of divine judgement on all oppressors. I release divine worms to eat up all satanic conspiracy against my handiwork. I abort every spiritual pregnancy over my life endeavours. My name is removed from the manifest of aero plane designed to crash land this year. My name is expunged from the register of tragedy this year in Jesus Christ name I declare. Amen

WEEK 36

This week, because the Lord lives, I shall live also. The joy of the Lord is my strength. I refuse to enroll in the college of anguish. I receive my graduation from the university of calamity. I divinely terminate the appointment of the lecturer marking my script of delays and frustration with immediate effect. The calendar of untimely death over my life has expired. I release confusion into evil association surmoned for my life. I cancel the time table of poverty over my life with the blood of Jesus Christ. I reschedule my enemies to useless assignments. My life is invisible to demonic observer. I withdraw all the ammunition I made available to my enemy. I shall never be spiritually amputated. I shall never be emotionally crippled. I shall never be financially dislocated. I shall never be maritally displaced by any strange woman / man. I shall never be stranded in life affairs. If evil is going ahead of me this week, the Lord will delay my footsteps such that I will not meet up with it. If calamity is coming behind me, the Lord will hasten my footsteps, and it will not catch up with me, in Jesus Christ marvelous name I confess. Amen.

WEEK 37

I make this heartfelt declaration this week that, in the name of Jesus Christ I am an over comer over the challenges of life. Wherever I have been crawling in the fulfillment of my destiny, I will walk this week. Wherever I was walking before, the time has come for me to begin to run!. Evil seed planted by fear, will not germinate in my life. My oppressors must be disgraced, by the armies of Heaven. I am delivered from the power of wasters. I am freed from the grip of delays and disappointment. My blessings swallowed by satanic powers, must be vomited by fire this week. I release paralysis on all powers, that are bent on doing me and my family harm. I return to the sender, every arrow of destruction fired at me. My right hand will never be converted to the left hand in Jesus Christ name. I burn satanic letter against my promotion. I divide the tongues of my enemies after the order of the tower of Babel. I see my foes becoming my footstool this blessed week. I will experience victory in every area of my life. I expose all my attackers, hiding within the tower of friendship to the firing squad of the Host of Heaven, I command heavenly worms to eat up all my adversaries hiding under the canopy of colleagues. My name will become thunder in the mouth of those calling it for evil purposes this week in Jesus Christ name I declare. Amen.

WEEK 38

Father, in Jesus Christ name, I thank you for the gift of life. You have given me in Christ. This is my week of concrete and tangible evidence. I will never be involved in the accident of life. I will not be located by demonic stray bullet of delays and stagnation. I will not download confusion from the computer of life. I will not be inducted into the hall of shame and ridicule. Alarm of danger will not sound in my life this week. Rain of tragedy will not fall upon me and my family. Wind of affliction will not blow over my marriage and health. I am sentenced to life enjoyment of God's abundance. I am condemned to show forth the praises of God who loved me and deliver me from the power of darkness. I am acquitted from evil gang – up. I am discharged from satanic conspiracy. I am bailed out of evil network by the blood of Jesus Christ. Satanic judgement over my life is overruled by the mercy of God. My eyes will never shed tears of sorrow. My eyes shall never run dry of joyful tears of astounding testimonies. My ears must receive good news from within and outside this blessed country. My mouth shall declare the goodness of God in the land of the living. My life shall reflect the glory and splendour of God. The beauty of Jesus Christ must be seen in my life and business this week, in Jesus sweetest name I confess. Amen

WEEK 39

Behold what manner of love God has bestowed on me and my family members. I boldly declare that, as vehicle queue up in the filling stations, so shall the angels of God queue up to refill my life with God's abundance. My evidence of glad tidings, must manifest this week. My prayers shall not enter satanic voice mail of long sufferings. I will not chicken out of Christian glorious adventures because of satanic weapon of discouragement. I will not be frustrated in life ambitions. My spiritual life shall surely stand the test of time. The fountains of my life shall never dry up from the Source of Life. The fallow ground of my life, shall receive the dew of Heaven this week. My heavens shall open by fire of God. I disconnect the transformer supplying the light of my glorious destiny to my enemies by my confession of faith, I blow up the transmitter relaying evil news about my life and career. I abort spiritual pregnancy over my endeavour. I will not enroll in the institution of lamentations. I receive my graduation from the university of pain and anguish. I close up every tap of sorrow over my life and family. I block every pipe bringing water of stagnation into my life. I shall not be confined to the wheel chair of set back. My advancement in life shall never be limited by satanic bumps of household wickedness, in Jesus wonderful name I confess. Amen

WEEK 40

Father Lord, I thank You for the wonder working power in your Word. I release myself to the Holy Spirit for partnership this week. My glorious manifestation will surprise even my enemies. Your anointing upon my life will proudly announce your great works in me this week. I am placed above every incident of sorrow. Accidental arrows that fly by day or night will never touch me or any member of my family. Whatsoever that is killing others cannot kill me, because of your unction upon my life. My glorious future is secured in Christ Jesus. I am the head among my equals. My works this week has no choice other than to greatly succeed. I will not sell my property for food. I recover now all that I have lost in life in the times of ignorance by the power of Holy Ghost. I receive divine wisdom and understanding to excel above my contemporaries. Inspired thoughts and creative mind are my portion in Christ. I over come tension because of the anointing of Holy Spirit upon my life. I hook up to God's internet and receive every information about my colourful destiny. I download obedience and faithfulness. I download fear of God and holy living. The unclear picture of my future will receive divine light and direction this week of divine encounter, in Jesus Christ name I declare.

WEEK 41

Dear Lord Jesus Christ, let the confession of my mouth and the meditation of my heart this week be acceptable to You my Lord and my redeemer. I refuse to live my life on the platform of trial and error. I will never sleep on the mattress of confusion. I will never wake up in the land of the dead. Common troubles will not be my portion and that of my family. I am confident that I will not miss my way in the affairs of life, because I have the Way and the Life guiding me. Nobody will exploit me again. I will not be short changed in the congregation of people that matters in the society. Evil hold up will not hinder my aspirations. From today, I welcome everyone that will bring success into my life. I reject those that will bring road block to my glorious expectations. Wherever my case is discussed this week, my divine supporters will overshadow my collective opposers. No devil will be able to stop my stepping from shame into noticeable fame. No power shall be able to stop my movement from ridiculous into miraculous. My season of celebration and recognition has come. People will celebrate with me because of God's favour that will be so astoundingly shown in my life. I will award the contract of Halleluyah shouting to every one around me because of God's timely visitation. In Jesus Christ name I declare. Amen

WEEK 42

God is not a man that He should lie, nor the son of man, that He should repent. God has spoken once, I have heard twice, that all power belongs to God. Therefore, this week, I believe every Word of God, and since by two immutable things, it is impossible for God to lie, every promise of God, for my life, will come to pass in Jesus Christ name. I now stand on the victory of Christ over Satan and his falling agents. The sons of those who afflicted me shall come bending low to me. All those who despised me shall bow down at my feet. I am the tree of glory planted by the Lord. I shall be called the city of the Lord I shall be decked with beauty. I shall be clothe with honour. I shall eat honey out of the rock of life. I shall surely reach my promised land of breakthroughs. Though I may have been forsaken. God will make me an eternal glory. Though I may have been hated, I shall be made an eternal joy, in the hand of the Lord. I shall eat the riches of the Gentiles. I shall boast myself in their glory, because God has remembered me. Every one shall see, and also acknowledge that I am the seed, which the Lord has blessed, in the most precious name of Jesus Christ. Amen.

WEEK 43

In the name of Immortal, invisible God only wise Jesus Christ, I will access the glorious light of God by His gracious mercy this week. The praise of His great name shall continually be on my lips. As I bow in penitence beneath His feet I will sue for His mercy. I will bless the Lord for His ceaseless care and love over me and my family this week. I will forever appreciate the wonder working power in His Word and blood. The Lord will surely be my everlasting portion and more than friend or life to me. I will closely walk with my Saviour on my pilgrim journey this week. I will not seek for ease or worldly pleasure in the affairs of life. The Lord will flood my heart this week with the light of heaven. The darkness of the earth shall not have power over me and my family. All things will surely work together for good for me in the issues of life this week. I will be protected from the snares of the fowler and from noisome pestilence by the power in the blood of Jesus Christ. The Lord will bring me to a place of maturity and deeper walk with Him this week. I will never be left alone nor forsaken in the battles of life. The angels of the Lord shall keep charge over me and my endeavours this week. I will dwell in the secret place of the Most High God and consciously abide under the shadows of His wings.

WEEK 44

Father, in the name of Jesus Christ, I thank you for the salvation of my soul. I bless your Holy name for your divine purpose for my life. I give you praise for fighting for me against my accusers. You are worthily adored for your wonderful love shown to me and my family. I thank you for your unfailing sure promises. I glorify your name that is highly exalted and greatly magnified. Thank you Father for giving us your Son, Jesus Christ as a propitiation for our sins. I bless the name of the Lord for the willingness and eagerness of Jesus Christ to lay down His life for the ransom of my soul. To God be the glory for leaving His precious and sweet Holy Spirit in the world to lead us to the cross. I thank you Jesus for your abiding presence in my life and family. I praise the beauty of Holiness for making things in my life, family and career beautiful in His time. The Lord will give me peace by all means this week. The Lord will calm the turbulent waves and the roars of life sea in my life this week. The boat of my life shall not capsize in the midst of life challenges. I will not wander in the wilderness of stubbornness like the children of Israel. My red sea must give way to a dry land of glorious path way. The Lord will arise in my life for signs and wonders this blessed week in Jesus priceless name.

WEEK 45

This week, Father, let the confession of my mouth and the meditation of my heart be acceptable to you in Jesus mighty name. I now put on righteousness of God as a clothing. My confession will provoke something good in the spirit realm. My best days are not behind me, they are right now ahead, ready to manifest this week. I see it, I feel it and I begin to live it out. People that matters in the society will be divinely connected to me effortlessly. They will cause me to experience mighty outpouring of God's blessings. This week, I shall not be a failure in the challenges of life. I am wonderfully made to display the beauty of my Maker. I am fearfully crafted to show forth the wonders of my Creator. I am gloriously packaged to be a blessing and an encouragement to my generation. I pronounce victory of Jesus Christ over the affairs of my life. I have been divinely chosen to be a winner. I am an high flyer achiever in the issues of life. I am a reigning champion in the battles of life. I am a success in the efforts of life. I am a pace setter in good things of life. I am a peace maker because the Prince of Peace lives inside of me. I am now unstoppable by the congregation of dark powers. I shall not die like a smoke. I choose to live as king and priest of the Most High God, because my Redeemer is alive for evermore. It is well with my soul, in Jesus name I make this declaration. Amen.

WEEK 46

Father, guide and instruct me, the way I should go this week, to generate outstanding results in the affairs of life, in Jesus Christ name. Unlike the barren fig tree, I am fertile and productive. I am fruitful in every area of my life. |All through this week, my life will make Heaven to rejoice., I shall fulfill God's ordained expectation of me. Every one that look up to m for good will never be disappointed. My enemies will not entangle me with selfish decision that will misdirect my colourful destiny. No weapon fashioned against me shall prosper. I cancel weapon of business failure. I reject weapon of academic rustication and dislocation. I refuse weapon of relationship breakdown. I destroy weapons of instability and confusion in my life. I will not be located. By arrow of miscarriage in my business and family. I abort every pregnancy of poverty in my life. I confess the conception of my promotion. I affirm the springing forth of my breakthroughs. I release myself from any demonic power holding me captive. I am free from demonic slavery. I am an heir of salvation. I have the spirit of over taker. I pursue and overtake the hijackers of my blessings. I receive divine power to excel in the affairs of life this week. I have the courage to break new ground in righteousness. The hidden potentials of God in me will manifest out this week by fire, in Jesus Christ name I confess. Amen

WEEK 47

I confess that this week, the Holy Spirit shall incubate my whole life against bewitchment. Every of my innate potential declared dead by my enemies shall live again by the resurrection power of Jesus Christ. This week, through the wisdom of God, I will build my life of peace and harmony. By the understanding of God's will, my life purpose shall be established. By the knowledge of God's heart beat, my chambers shall be filled with precious and pleasant riches. I receive double restoration for all the years that locust and caterpillars has eaten up in my life. I break every covenant of shame and disgrace over my life. I disgrace every serpent and scorpion power militating against my life. I command every dumb and deaf spirit to loose their hold over the aspiration of my life. I refuse to be pulled out of my miracle arena by satanic deceit. I return back to sender, every premature breakthroughs fashioned against my career and business. I now move from minimum to maximum. My miracle shall be energized to maturity this week by the power made the heavens and the earth. The cloud of glory that will envelope my dwellings place by day and cloud of fire by night. The agenda of wicked powers shall not come to pass over my life and family, in Jesus Christ name I make my declarations. Amen.

WEEK 48

Father, unto You that is able to do exceedingly far above all that we ask or think through the power that works in us, be all the glory, honour, praise and majesty for ever in Jesus Christ name. I will not fail You this week. My loyalty to Heaven will not be questioned or compromised. I will be careful to return glory to you God for your operations in my life this week. I command every life protocols to be adjusted to fit the fulfillment of my glorious destiny. I am God's dependable representative for this generation. I will shine as diamond. I receive enough spiritual strength to conquer every Goliath that will defy the army of God's testimonies in my life this week. I refuse to wear any iron boot of stagnation. I will never use satanic make – up of deceit. I will never wear devilish attachment of hatred on the hair of my glory. I will never apply the satanic manicure of bondage to my life. I will not use the pedicure of stagnation. I receive sensitivity and strength from the Holy Spirit. I have divine boldness to carry out God's instruction to the letter. The anointing of God on me will attract divine favour into my life. Never again will I be counted among the invalids of life. Long time affliction in my life has come to an abrupt end now in Jesus Christ name. I will not b displaced in my palace of glory. It will never take eternity for my testimonies to fully manifest. This is my week of astounding results. It is my season of undeniable proofs of God's faithfulness in this land of the living, in Jesus Christ name I declare. Amen.

WEEK 49

This week, heaven will attend speedily to my confession in the name of Jesus Christ. I yield to the superiority of God, so that His best riches will be mine. I plan my life around God's will. I will never be a liability to any one in life. I will never be afraid of my responsibilities this week. I receive the answer to any question of my life from the Word of God. I live in the supernatural empowerment of God. I maintain unbroken fellowship with the Holy Spirit. I manifest the nature of God's kingdom in my life. Every good thing that is in short supply in my life before now must overflow this week in Jesus Christ name. I will never be too slow to accomplish divine assignment for my life. For every disappointment I had last week, I receive fresh and sure appointment that will move me to my next higher level in life. Strange doors in righteousness shall be opened unto me this week. I silence every voice of opposition against my peace. I stop the mouth of accusation crying against the fulfillment of my destiny. I am the beloved of God, by virtue of Jesus Christ sacrifice for me on the cross of Calvary. I am the joy of many generations, in Jesus Christ name I confess. Amen.

WEEK 50

Father, I thank you for the gift of this new week of pleasant surprises. It is my new week of divine opportunities. I will wash my feet with the butter of life. The rock of life will pour me out rivers of oil. I will dwell in the city of abundance, through the gateway of thanksgiving and the court of praise. I will prepare my seat of honour in the street of humility. This week, the ungodly men of life will see me and hid themselves because the light of God in me will expose their wickedness. The princes of life will refrain from talking to me in amazement because of the wisdom of God that will manifest in my relationship with them. They will lay their hands on their mouth in wonders of the goodness of God to me. The noble men of life will hold their peace. Their tongues will cleave to the roof of their mouth in utter disbelief, because of my divine transformation. The ear of men will hear me, it will bless me. The eyes of men will see me and give witness to me. I will deliver the crying poor. I will rescue the fatherless. Those who have none to help them, shall rejoice at my appearing to them this week. The blessing of him that is ready to perish will come upon me. I will cause the widow's heart to sing for joy. The zeal of the Lord of Host will perform this on my behalf, as I diligently listen to His voice, in Jesus Christ march less name I declare. Amen.

WEEK 51

The name of the Lord is a strong tower. It is sufficient for me to trust in this week. I will put on righteousness and it will clothe me. My judgement will be as a robe and a diadem. I will be eyes to the blinds of life. I will be feet to the lames and cripple of life. I will be a father to the poor by the help of God. I will be a mother to the feeble of life. The cause which I know not, I will search out by the grace and the leading of the Lord. I will break the jaws of the wicked. I will by these deliberate actions multiply my days as the sand of the sea shore. My root will spread out by the waters of life. The dew of heaven will lay all night upon my branch. The glory of God will be fresh on me like the morning waters taken from the river. My bow of war will be renewed in my hand. Unto me men will give hear this week. They shall cravingly wait for my encouragement. They will also keep silence when they hear my counsel. They will not be able to speak after my words again. My speech will drop upon them as the dew of Hermon. Men will wait for me as the earth for the rain. Women will open their mouth wide as for the latter rain. The light of my countenance will not be cast down. I will dwell as a king in the army of men. As I call for one man, many men will rush to attend to me. I will never lack help in the affairs of life, in Jesus name I confess. Amen.

WEEK 52

Oh God, my heart is fixed on You alone this week. I will sing of your mercy and give praise to your Holy name. I will then be exalted above my detractors. The mouth of the wicked will not be opened against me, I shall not be compassed about with the words of hatred. My adversaries will never reward me again evil for good. The days of my enemies are shortened on the surface of the earth. The children of my oppressors will become vagabonds in life. My detractors will seek their bread out of desolate places. No one will ever extend mercy to my enemies. The waters of life will not overwhelm me and my family. I shall not be given to my enemies as a prey. My soul is escaped as a bird out of the snare of the fowler of life. The trap of my adversaries against my destiny will catch its owners. Every lying in wait of the enemies against my breakthroughs shall result into their lying in state for their burial. My heaven shall no more become brass. My earth shall no longer produce thistles and thorns. The rod of the wicked shall not rest upon my lots in life. The good Lord that kept the lot of Abraham in Sodom and Gommorah will keep my lots in this perilous generation. My captivity is turned again by the Lord. It is my season to reap in joy all that I have sown in tears. I will surely and doubtless rejoice this week. In Jesus Christ name I declare. Amen

WEEK 53

It shall come to pass this last week of the year, that as I hearken diligently to the voice of the Lord my God, I will be blessed in the city. I will be blessed in the field. The fruit of my body will be blessed. My basket and my store shall be abundantly blessed. I am blessed as I come in. I am blessed as I go out. My enemies shall be smitten before my face. As they come against me in one way, they shall flee before me seven ways. This week, the multitudes of camels shall cover me. The flocks of Kedar shall gathered together to me. The rams of Nebaioth shall minister to me. The isles of abundance shall surely wait for me. The sons of strangers shall build my walls. Their kings shall minister to me. My gates of colourful destiny shall be opened continually. Men will bring unto me the forces of the Gentiles. The glory of Lebanon shall come to me. I will suck the breast of the kings of life. I will drink also the milk of the Gentiles. Violence has ended in my life and my family. There shall no more be wasting nor destruction within my borders. My walls shall be called Salvation. My gate is surnamed Praise. My sun shall no more go down. My sun will keep on shining until perfection of the son of man. My moon shall not withdraw itself. The star of my glory will not be hijacked by star hunters of life. The Lord has become my everlasting light. The days of my mourning has come to an abrupt end. My best days are happening from now. In Jesus Christ name I make this confession of faith. Amen.

Please do get in touch with us and let us know how this inspired booklet has been of great blessings to you as you share your glorious testimonies with us. The good Lord Jesus Christ Himself will take all the glory, honour and praise. You can call and text us on Telephone: +2349095626923; +2347013705660, or +2348074548381 or better still e-mail us at: commissioned2encourageu@yahoo.co.uk or greathousemission@yahoo.com:

Printed in the United States
By Bookmasters